First Atlas

DP
DEMPSEY PARR

This edition published by Dempsey Parr, 1999
Dempsey Parr is an imprint of Parragon

Parragon
Queen Street House, 4 Queen Street, Bath BA1 1HE, UK.

Copyright © Parragon 1998

2 4 6 8 10 9 7 5 3 1

Produced by Miles Kelly Publishing Ltd,
Bardfield Centre, Great Bardfield, Essex, CM7 4SL

Editor: Sean Connolly
Cartographic Editor: Keith Lye
Design: Full Steam Ahead
Artwork Commissioning: Branka Surla
Project Manager: Kate Miles
Additional help from Ian Paulyn and Lynne French

ISBN 1 84084 442 6

Printed in Spain

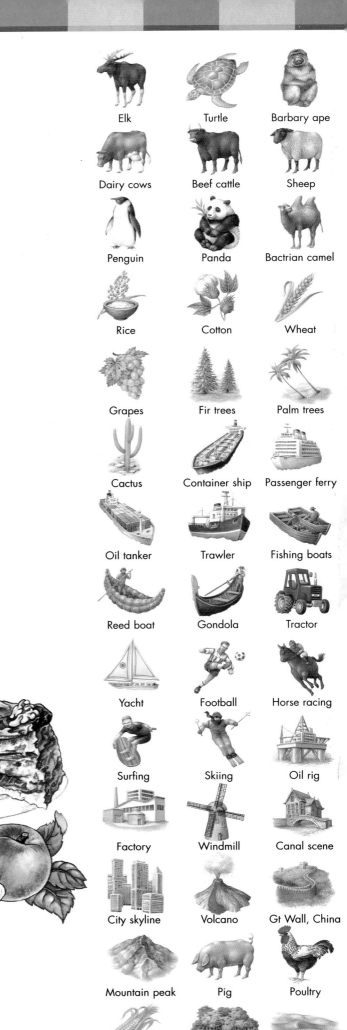

Elk   Turtle   Barbary ape

Dairy cows   Beef cattle   Sheep

Penguin   Panda   Bactrian camel

Rice   Cotton   Wheat

Grapes   Fir trees   Palm trees

Cactus   Container ship   Passenger ferry

Oil tanker   Trawler   Fishing boats

Reed boat   Gondola   Tractor

Yacht   Football   Horse racing

Surfing   Skiing   Oil rig

Factory   Windmill   Canal scene

City skyline   Volcano   Gt Wall, China

Mountain peak   Pig   Poultry

Maize   Rainforest   Sand dunes

Tourism

Icons
These little pictures on the maps
give you all sorts of extra
information about a country.
Some of them show buildings.
Others show landscapes,
animals or plants. Some show
the kind of work people do, or
how they spend their free time.

Contents

Introduction

Earth Facts

The world we live in is a planet, a huge ball of rock which flies through space. It is called Earth. The Earth travels around our local star, which is called the Sun. As it travels, it spins around and around. It stays on course because it is pulled toward the Sun by a force called gravity. The Earth is one of nine planets that circle the Sun. It is also the only planet on which living things are known to exist.

When we see pictures of Earth taken from out in space, it looks beautiful. We can see the bright blue of the oceans. We can see the brown of the rocks and soil that make up big areas of land. These are called continents. We can see swirling white patterns, too. These are clouds, made up of tiny drops of water. They float in the air that surrounds the planet. Air and water make it possible for us to live on Earth.

Did you know?
- The Equator is an imaginary line drawn around the middle of the Earth. It is 24,887 miles long.
- The top and bottom points of the planet are called the North and South Poles. A line drawn around the world passing through these two points is just a bit shorter than the Equator.
- That means that the world isn't perfectly round. Its shape is ever so slightly squashed!

Deserts are very dry areas of rock, stones, or sand. This desert is part of **Death Valley**, in California.

High mountain ranges are covered by snow and ice. These are the **Andes** mountains, in South America.

The giant clam is one of the fascinating and varied sorts of sea life found on the **Great Barrier Reef**, off the coast of Queensland in Australia.

What is a map?

A map is a plan showing the planet's surface. The Earth's surface is curved, so it can only be shown properly on a round globe. Maps are normally on paper, and so the surface has to be shown as if it were flat.

Many maps show the lie of the land. You can see which areas are low and which are high. You can pick out mountain peaks, coasts and rivers, lakes and seas. These are called natural features. Some maps just show the borders of countries, states, and provinces. Some show cities, roads, and railroad lines. The maps in this atlas show the land and coastlines as well as national borders and cities.

Read the map
This map is of Japan. What are the names of the four main islands? Is the land mostly flat or mountainous?

Spot the mountain
Maps use little badges called symbols. A small black triangle means 'mountain'. Look for the name of the peak and its height in feet above sea level. Other symbols are shown below.

Towns and cities
Towns and cities are shown by round dots. Each country's chief city, or capital, is shown by a square.

JAPAN

HOKKAIDO

Kuril Is. (Russia)

Asahi Mt. 7,511 ft

Sapporo

Kitakami

Sendai

Mito

HONSHU

Tokyo

Yokohama

Mt. Fuji 12,385 ft

Kyoto

Nagoya

Kobe

Osaka

Hiroshima

PACIFIC OCEAN

Kitakyushu

Fukuoka

SHIKOKU

Kii Channel

KYUSHU

Where in the world?
Look for the little round maps to see just where each map fits on to the globe as a whole

Key to symbols
capital city ■
city or town ●
mountain ▲
national border ——
coastline
river
lake
highlands
plains

Countries of the World

Bolivian women come into market, high in the Andes mountains of South America.

There are 192 countries in the world that are called independent. That means that they rule themselves. Many other lands are called dependencies or colonies, which means that they are ruled by other countries. The number of countries changes all the time, as some split up or else join together to make new nations. The world's biggest country is the Russian Federation, and the world's smallest is Vatican City, which fits inside Rome, the capital of Italy. The country with the most people is China. Nobody at all lives in Antarctica, apart from a few visiting scientists, but several countries claim parts of this land.

The ancestors of the **Araucanian peoples** lived in Chile long before their land was invaded by Europeans.

GREENLAND

Baffin Bay

Chukchi Sea

Beaufort Sea

Bering Strait

Davis Strait

Denmark Strait

ICELAND

Hudson Bay

IRELAN

Gulf of Alaska

ALEUTIAN ISLANDS

C A N A D A

Newfoundland

N O R T H

PORTU

A T L A N T I C

PORTU

O C E A N

MOROC

UNITED STATES OF AMERICA

CANARY ISLANDS

WESTERN SAHARA

Gulf of Mexico

HAWAIIAN ISLANDS

BAHAMAS

CUBA

MEXICO

W E S T

JAMAICA

HAITI

DOMINICAN REPUBLIC

PUERTO RICO

I N D I E S

MAURITAN

BELIZE

Caribbean Sea

SENEGAL

GUATEMALA

HONDURAS

GAMBIA

EL SALVADOR

NICARAGUA

GUINEA-BISSAU

GUI

COSTA RICA

TRINIDAD & TOBAGO

SIERRA LEON

PANAMA

VENEZUELA

GUYANA

SURINAM

FRENCH GUIANA

LIB

COLOMBIA

GALAPAGOS ISLANDS

ECUADOR

S O U T

B R A Z I L

A T L A N

PERU

O C E A

BOLIVIA

PARAGUAY

CHILE

URUGUAY

ARGENTINA

FALKLAND/MALVINAS ISLANDS

South Georgia

North Americans like to show off their **cowboy** skills at shows called rodeos.

Over 150 different peoples live in the **Russian Federation**. Many have their own languages and way of life.

A father holds his son at **Lijiang**, a town in the mountainous part of Yunnan province, southwest China.

Movement, color and costume are all part of traditional dance in **India**.

SVALBARD

ZEMLYA FRANTSA IOSIFA

SEVERNAYA ZEMLYA

Laptev Sea

NOVOSIBIRSKIVE OSTROVO

East Siberian Sea

Novaya Zemlya

Barents Sea

Kara Sea

Norwegian Sea

SWEDEN FINLAND

NORWAY

ESTONIA

North Sea

DENMARK LATVIA

ED

OM

Baltic Sea

LITHUANIA

RUSSIA

ETHERLANDS

BELARUS

GERMANY POLAND

LGIUM CZECH

LUXEMBOURG REP. SLOVAKIA

AUSTRIA

UKRAINE

ITZERLAND HUNGARY

MOLDOVA

RANCE SLOVENIA ROMANIA

CROATIA

NDORRA BOSNIA-HERZEGOVINA YUGOSLAVIA Black Sea

ITALY MACEDONIA BULGARIA

ALBANIA ARMENIA AZERBAIJAN

GREECE TURKEY

Caspian Sea

GEORGIA

UZBEKISTAN

TURKMENISTAN TAJIKISTAN

KAZAKHSTAN

MONGOLIA

RUSSIA

Sea of Okhotsk

Bering Sea

TUNISIA

Mediterranean Sea

CYPRUS SYRIA

LEBANON

ISRAEL IRAQ IRAN

JORDAN

Aral

KYRGYZSTAN

AFGHANISTAN

CHINA

NORTH KOREA

SOUTH KOREA JAPAN

Sea of Japan

Yellow Sea

ERIA LIBYA EGYPT SAUDI ARABIA QATAR

UNITED ARAB EMIRATES

PAKISTAN

NEPAL BHUTAN

BANGLADESH

East China Sea

LI NIGER CHAD

OMAN

INDIA

BURMA

TAIWAN

KINA SUDAN ERITREA YEMEN

SO

Red Sea

Gulf of Aden

LAOS

HONG KONG

Philippine Sea

NIGERIA

CENTRAL AFRICAN REPUBLIC

ETHIOPIA

Bay of Bengal

THAILAND

VIETNAM

South China Sea

CAMBODIA

PHILIPPINES

CAMEROON SOMALIA

EQUATORIAL GUINEA

GABON CONGO ZAIRE UGANDA KENYA

f of nea

SRI LANKA

BRUNEI

MALAYSIA

Celebes Sea

RWANDA BURUNDI

TANZANIA

EAST INDIES

MELANESIA

INDONESIA

PAPUA NEW GUINEA

SOLOMON ISLANDS

ANGOLA ZAMBIA MALAWI

INDIAN OCEAN

NAMIBIA ZIMBABWE

MOZAMBIQUE

Mozambique Channel

MADAGASCAR MAURITIUS

RÉUNION

Coral Sea

VANUATU

FIJI

NEW CALEDONIA

BOTSWANA

SWAZILAND

LESOTHO

SOUTH AFRICA

AUSTRALIA

Tasman Sea

North I.

NEW ZEALAND

South I.

The **Masai** people live on the hot, dusty grasslands of East Africa. The men wear cloaks. The women wear wide collars made of beads.

Feathers, paint, and shells are worn for local festivals in the hills and forests of **Papua New Guinea**.

7

Scandinavia and Finland

The Baltic and the North Sea are divided by two long arms of the European mainland, which together are known as Scandinavia. The southern arm is called Jutland. Along with several large islands it makes up a country called Denmark. This land is flat and green. Its farms produce butter and bacon.

The other long arm of land stretches down from the Arctic. Its coastline is ragged, with deep sea inlets called fjords in the west. Mountains run down from north to south. There are big forests and thousands of lakes, sparkling blue in summer, but frozen over during the harsh northern winter. The western lands belong to Norway and the eastern lands to Sweden. Oil is taken from beneath the North Sea, metals from the land, and timber from the forests. The eastern shores of the Baltic Sea are taken up by Finland, a land of forests and lakes stretching to the borders of Russia.

These soldiers are on duty outside **Amalienborg Castle** in **Denmark**. Their job is to guard the life of the Danish queen.

RUSSIA

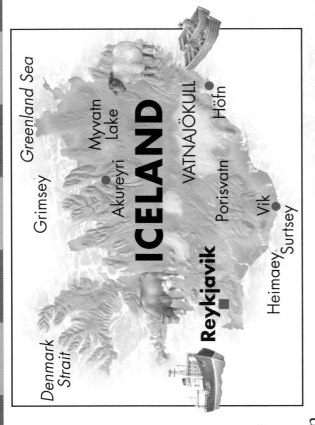

Greenland Sea

Grimsey

Myvatn Lake

Akureyri

ICELAND

VATNAJÖKULL

Höfn

Þorisvatn

Reykjavík

Vík

Heimaey

Surtsey

Denmark Strait

North Cape

Hammerfest

LAPLAND

Narvik

Kiruna

▲ Mt. Kebnekaise 6,924 ft

LOFOTEN VESTERÅLE

Luleå

Oulu

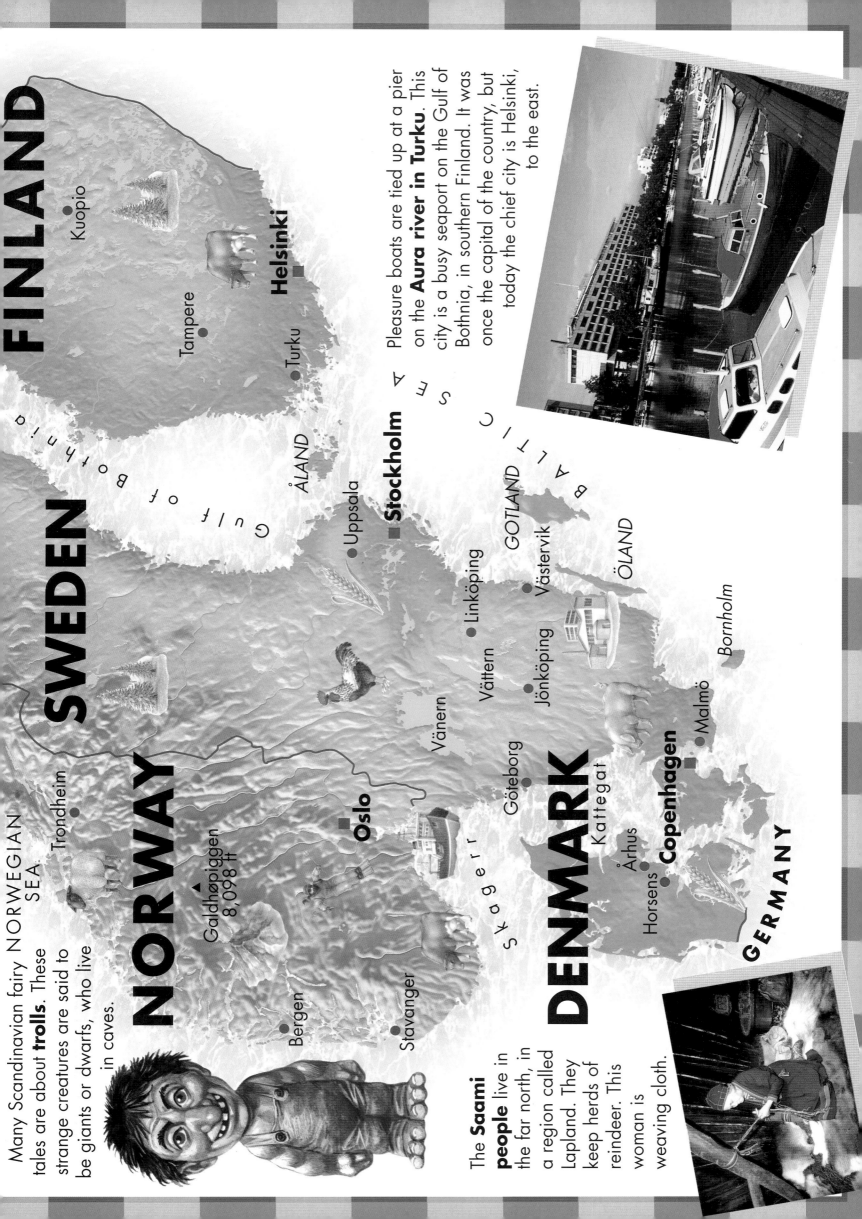

FINLAND

Kuopio

Tampere

Helsinki

Turku

Pleasure boats are tied up at a pier on the **Aura river in Turku**. This city is a busy seaport on the Gulf of Bothnia, in southern Finland. It was once the capital of the country, but today the chief city is Helsinki, to the east.

Gulf of Bothnia

SWEDEN

ÅLAND

Uppsala

Stockholm

BALTIC SEA

GOTLAND

Västervik

Linköping

Vättern

Jönköping

ÖLAND

Vänern

Bornholm

Göteborg

Malmö

NORWAY

Trondheim

Galdhøpiggen 8,098 ft

Oslo

Bergen

Stavanger

Skagerr

DENMARK

Kattegat

Århus

Horsens

Copenhagen

GERMANY

Many Scandinavian fairy tales are about **trolls**. These strange creatures are said to be giants or dwarfs, who live in caves.

NORWEGIAN SEA.

The **Saami people** live in the far north, in a region called Lapland. They keep herds of reindeer. This woman is weaving cloth.

Low Countries

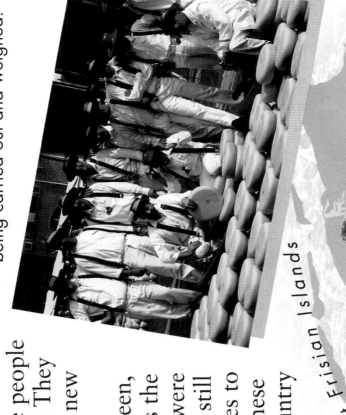

Alkmaar is a town in the North Holland region of the Netherlands. Tourists like to visit its famous **cheese market**, and watch the big, round cheeses being carried out and weighed.

The Netherlands and Belgium border the North Sea and are very low lying. For hundreds of years the people there have fought against floods and storms. They have learned to fill in coastal areas to make new farmland, called polder.

The lands near the coast are flat and green, drained by canals and by great rivers such as the Rhine, the Schelde, and the Meuse. Windmills were once used to pump out the wet fields, and may still be seen today. In southern Belgium the land rises to a chain of wooded hills called the Ardennes. These stretch southward into Luxembourg, a tiny country with rich farmland.

The Netherlands is famous for its cheeses, its vegetables, cut flowers, and electrical goods. Belgium produces steel and machinery. Luxembourg produces wine and is a center of business.

The lowlands region is home to several peoples, including Frisians, Dutch, Flemings, and Walloons.

This is the **Atomium**, a strange-looking landmark in Brussels, the capital of Belgium. It was built forty years ago for a big international fair.

Amsterdam, the capital of the Netherlands, is built around a network of canals. The Prinsengracht runs through the old part of the city, which was built in the 1600s.

NETHERLANDS

Groningen

Enschede

West Frisian Islands

Waddenzee

IJsselmeer

Haarlem ■ **Amsterdam**

GERMANY

GERMANY

LUXEMBOURG

Luxembourg

Delicious **white** and **dark chocolates** are made by hand in Belgium. The country also produces cooked meats such as pâtés, and strong beers.

Arnhem

Nijmegen

Maas

Eindhoven

Waal

Lek

Tilburg

Maastricht

Rotterdam

The Hague

Botrange 694m

Liège

Meuse

ARDENNES MOUNTAINS

Antwerp

Brussels

BELGIUM

Sambre Namur

Charleroi

Ghent

Bruges

Schelde

Mons

FRANCE

Ostend

In springtime many fields in the Netherlands turn yellow, orange, red, or pink as **tulips** come into bloom. The Dutch sell bulbs and also cut flowers to many parts of the world.

Belgian towns such as Bruges have been making **beautiful lace** for over 400 years. The thread is wound around pins on a cushion.

These tiles were made in **Delft**, a town in the South Holland region of the Netherlands. Delft is famous for its beautiful pottery, which is often colored in shades of blue.

British Isles

The British Isles lie off the mainland of Europe. Ocean currents and winds keep the weather mild and moist. The largest island is Great Britain, which is made up of three countries joined together in a United Kingdom. These are England, Scotland, and Wales. The second biggest island is called Ireland. The northern part of this is governed as part of the United Kingdom, but most of it is a separate country called the Republic of Ireland.

England has rich farmland in the south and bleak moors in the north. Both Scotland and Wales include highlands where sheep or cattle are raised. Many islands lie to the west and to the north of Scotland. There are many large cities in Great Britain. The biggest of all is London, on the River Thames. The Irish capital is called Dublin. Ireland is a land of green fields, peat bogs, mountains, and rivers.

Bagpipes are played in the highlands of Scotland. Pipe music can be sad or stirring. Bagpipes are sometimes used by pop bands as well as by traditional pipers.

This brightly painted **longboat** is on the River Wey, in the southeast of England. Longboats like these were once used to transport pottery and other factory goods. Today they are mostly used for vacation cruises.

SHETLAND ISLANDS

ORKNEY ISLANDS

John o'Groats

N O R T H   S E A

Peterhead

Aberdeen

Dundee

Inverness

Perth

Loch Ness

Forth

Edinburgh

Glasgow

NORTH WEST

Ben Nevis 4,405 ft

SCOTLAND

Mallaig

Ayr

Skye

Islay

Newcastle upon Tyne

Lewis

OUTER HEBRIDES

INNER HEBRIDES

Londonderry

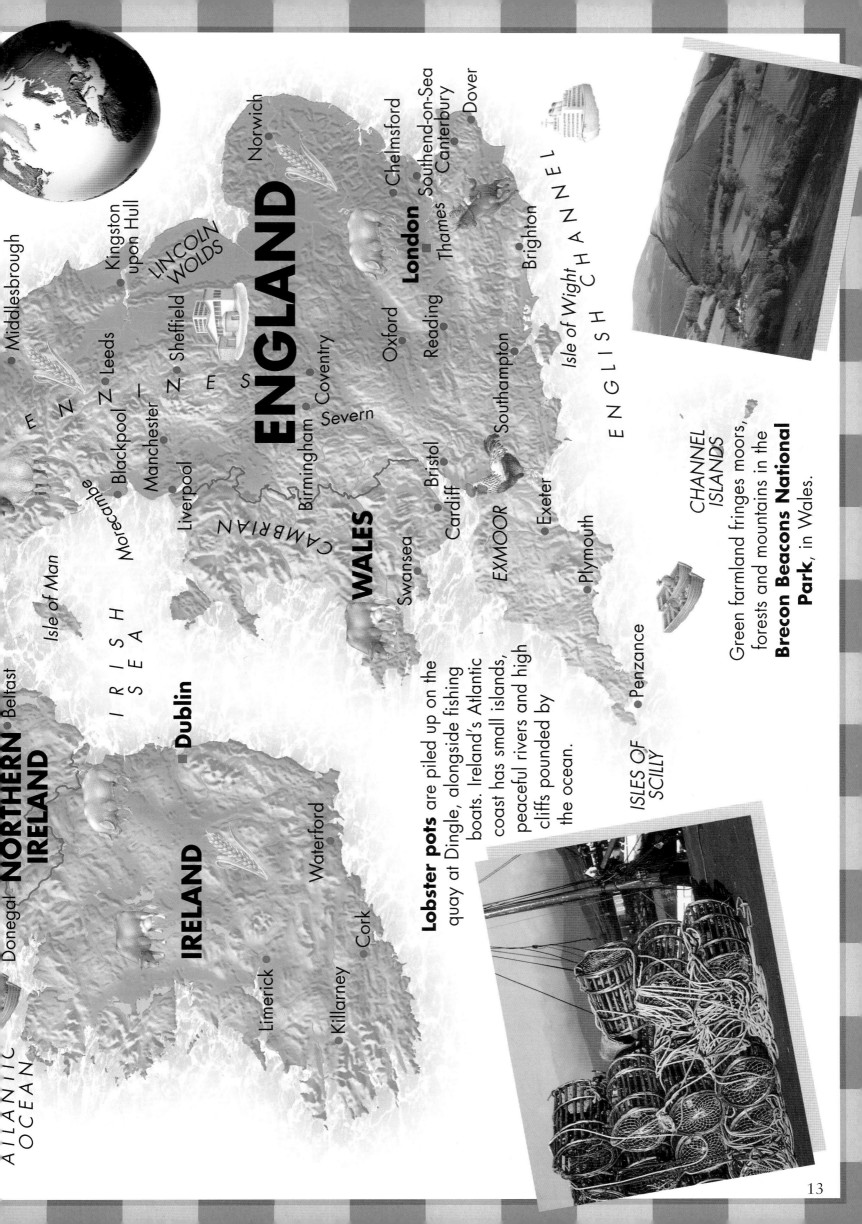

ATLANTIC OCEAN

Middlesbrough

NORTHERN IRELAND
Belfast

Donegal

Isle of Man

IRISH SEA

Dublin

IRELAND

Limerick

Killarney

Cork

Waterford

Lobster pots are piled up on the quay at Dingle, alongside fishing boats. Ireland's Atlantic coast has small islands, peaceful rivers and high cliffs pounded by the ocean.

Kingston upon Hull

LINCOLN WOLDS

Sheffield

Leeds

Blackpool

Manchester

Morecambe

Liverpool

ENGLAND

Norwich

Chelmsford

Coventry

Birmingham

Severn

London

Thames

Oxford

Reading

Southend-on-Sea

Canterbury

Dover

Brighton

Isle of Wight

ENGLISH CHANNEL

WALES

CAMBRIAN

Swansea

Cardiff

Bristol

Southampton

EXMOOR

Exeter

Plymouth

Penzance

ISLES OF SCILLY

CHANNEL ISLANDS

Green farmland fringes moors, forests and mountains in the **Brecon Beacons National Park**, in Wales.

France and Monaco

France lies at the center of western Europe. It is bordered by the Atlantic Ocean in the west and the Mediterranean Sea in the south. Two high mountain ranges, the Pyrenees and the Alps, divide France from Spain and Italy. In the north, a train tunnel beneath the Channel links the country to England.

The north of the country is mostly flat farmland. The River Seine flows through the French capital, Paris. To the south are the highlands of the Massif Central and the broad valley of the River Rhône.

French farmers grow apples and pears and make all sorts of cheeses. French wines and French cooking too are famous around the world. France makes cars and trains and fashionable clothes.

Monaco is a tiny country on the Mediterranean coast, famous for its gambling and motor racing.

One of the best ways of seeing Paris is by taking a boat trip on the **River Seine**. The city has fine cathedrals and churches, art galleries and museums, bars, and restaurants.

The **Eiffel Tower** soars above the center of Paris. It was built more than a hundred years ago.

Cherbourg

Le Havre

CHANNEL ISLANDS (UK)
St.-Malo

Brest

Le Mans

Loir

St. Nazaire

Tours

Nantes

Chatellerault

Poiters

F R

Cognac

BAY OF BISCAY)

CORSICA
Ajaccio
Bonifacio

Bordeaux

Garonne

Biarritz

Lourdes

SPAIN

Vines are being pruned in Alsace, a part of France that borders Germany. French grapes produce some of the world's best wines.

Calais
Boulogne
Lille

BELGIUM

LUXEMBOURG

GERMANY

Dieppe

Rouen

Seine

Reims

Marne

Meuse

Paris

Nancy

Strasbourg

Chartres

Moselle

Rhine

Orléans

Loire

Saône

Haute cuisine means high-quality cooking. French families love to eat well, either at home or in a restaurant.

SWITZERLAND

mussels

chicken

snails

A N C E

Saôn

Limoges

Clermont-Ferrand

Lyon

Rhône

Mont Blanc
4,807 m

fruit pie

MASSIF
CENTRAL

St.-Étienne

Grenoble

A
L
P
S

ITALY

Dordogne

Lot

Lot

Rhône

cheese

Avignon

Toulouse

Montpellier

MONACO
Nice
Cannes

Marseille
Toulon

Many rich people tie up their yachts at **Monte Carlo**, in Monaco. French ports such as Cannes and Nice also attract wealthy tourists.

Perpignan

ANDORRA

Germany and the Alps

NORTH SEA

EAST FRISIAN

Three small countries take in most of western Europe's highest mountain range, the Alps. They are Switzerland, Liechtenstein, and Austria. Here, snowy peaks and rivers of ice tower over green valleys, dark forests, and deep lakes. Wooden houses stand in Alpine meadows. They are covered with snow in winter, but are bright with flowers in summer. Languages spoken in the Alps include German, French, Romansh, and Italian.

The Alps stretch northward into southern Germany. Germany is a large country which lies at the heart of Europe. It has forests and steep river valleys, rolling heath, and flat plains. Sandy coasts border the North Sea and the Baltic Sea. Germany has many big cities, with factories producing cars, chemical products, and electrical goods, but it also has pretty villages dating back to the Middle Ages. The German language is spoken throughout, but with many different accents.

The **Matterhorn** is a great needle of rock and ice. It rises in the Swiss Alps, near the Italian border.

Hambu

Bremen

Weser

Hannover All

HARZ M

Rhine

Dortmund

Essen

Düsseldorf

Cologne (Köln)

Bonn

GERMA

Rhine

Frankfurt am Main

FRANCE

Rhine

BLACK FOREST

Stuttgart

Lake Constanc (Bodensee)

Zurich

LIECHTENSTE

Vaduz

Bern

SWITZERLAND

Lake Geneva

ALPS

Geneva

BALTIC SEA

Elbe

Berlin

POLAND

Elbe

•Leipzig

Weimar

•Dresden

NY

CZECH REPUBLIC

uremberg (Nürnberg)

Danube

Linz

Vienna

Danube

Munich (München)

Salzburg

AUSTRIA

Innsbruck

•Graz

SLOVENIA

Berlin is the capital of Germany. It is an exciting, artistic city, but in the last hundred years it has suffered terribly from wars and troubles. This is the **Reichstag**, built a hundred years ago for the German parliament.

Lights shine out over the snowy forest at Lech, in **Vorarlberg**, western Austria. The Alpine lands attract walkers in summer and skiers in winter.

Munich is the chief town of Bavaria in southern Germany. During the autumn **Oktoberfest**, tourists join Bavarians in traditional dress to drink big glasses of the local beer.

Kaffee und Küchen—coffee and cakes—are a special treat in Germany and in the cafés of Vienna, the Austrian capital.

17

Spain and Portugal

The Iberian peninsula is a great block of land which juts out into the Atlantic Ocean. It is ringed by the snowy mountains of the Pyrenees, the Cantabrian ranges, and the Sierra Nevada. Much of it is dry and hot in summer. Rivers cross the western plains and flow into the Atlantic.

The region grows grapes for wine, olives, oranges, and cork. There are large fishing fleets. Factories produce cars and leather goods. Many tourists spend their vacations on the coasts.

There are three nations on the Iberian peninsula. The smallest is Andorra, high in the Pyrenees. Portugal, in the west, is a beautiful country with its own language. The largest country is Spain. Here, Spanish is spoken everywhere, but a number of other peoples have their own languages and way of life, including the Basques, Galicians, and Catalans. A fourth piece of land, Gibraltar in the far south, is a British colony.

Bay of Biscay

La Coruña

Gijón

CANTABRIAN

CAPE FINISTERRE

Vigo

Valladolid

Porto

Douro

PORTUGAL

Coimbra

Tajo

Tagus

Lisbon

Guadiana

Córdoba

Seville · Guadalquivir

Gulf of Cadiz

A thousand years ago, Arab peoples from North Africa ruled most of Spain. They were Muslims and built beautiful **mosques** such as this one in Cordoba.

Cádiz

Gibraltar (U.K.)

Strait of Gibraltar

18

Ronda is a small town of white houses in Andalucía, in southern Spain. It is built on the edge of towering cliffs which are linked by high bridges.

MOUNTAINS

Bilbao

Vitoria

FRANCE

PYRENEES

Pamplona

ANDORRA
Andorra la Vella

Ebro

Duero

Saragossa

Barcelona

S P A I N

Madrid

Menorca

Mallorca

Palma

Valencia

Ibiza

Spanish girls in traditional costume enjoy all the fun of the fair. Spain has many festivals called **fiestas**. Many of these celebrate Christian saints' days.

Alicante

La Carolina

Linares

Murcia

Guadiana

Granada

M E D I T E R R A N E A N   S E A

Portuguese food includes delicious seafood dishes, sardines, fruits, and wines. The drink port takes its name from the town of Oporto.

19

Garda is the largest lake in Italy. It is set among the high peaks of the Alps and has attracted tourists since the days of the ancient Romans.

Carnival is a festival held in the week before the Christian period of Lent. It is a time for parties and fancy dress. In Venice people wear masks and beautiful costumes and cloaks.

SLOVENIA

Trieste

Venice

San Marino

SAN MARINO

Po

Bologna

E

Florence

AUSTRIA

Verona

P

SWITZERLAND

Alps

Milan

Genoa

Pisa

A

ITALY

Vatican City
(in Rome)

Rome

N

N

Latina

TYRRHENIAN
SEA

Naples

S

Bari

Taranto

Sassari

MONACO

**Corsica
(France)**

FRANCE

Turin

Many famous cars are produced in Italy. They include the fast **Ferrari** sports car and racing cars as well as the Fiat range of family cars.

Italy and its Neighbors

Italy is a long strip of land stretching into the Mediterranean Sea. In the north are the Alps, a range of high mountains. Below these is a wide plain, crossed by the River Po.

The Appenine mountains run down the center of the country. Southern Italy includes large areas of dry scrubland. Volcanoes and earthquakes are common. Italy also includes the islands of Sicily and Sardinia.

Italy is the world's biggest wine producer and also exports many foods, including pasta, sauces, olives, and salami sausages. Factories in the north produce cars, clothes, and leather goods.

Inside Italy there are two other countries, tiny San Marino and also Vatican City, headquarters of the Roman Catholic Church. Another small country, Malta, lies to the south of Sicily.

Pisa is a town on the River Arno, in the Italian region of Tuscany. Medieval buildings around the central square include a cathedral, a building for baptisms and a famous bell tower which leans over sideways!

LIPARI ISLANDS

IONIAN SEA

Catania

SICILY

Palermo

Fishing boats are moored in the harbor of Valletta, the capital of **Malta**. This island nation lies to the south of Sicily.

MALTA

Italy is famous for making some of world's most delicious ice-creams. An ice-cream parlor is called a **gelateria**.

SARDINIA

Cagliari

21

Central Europe

Three small countries border the Baltic Sea. Estonia, Latvia, and Lithuania include large areas of forest, bog, and open farmland. Until the 1990s these Baltic lands were a part of Russia, which was then called the Soviet Union. Poland, to the south, is a much larger country, lying on a wide open plain between Germany in the west and Belarus and Ukraine in the east. In the south are wooded hills and the high peaks of the Tatra mountains, on the Slovakian border. The Czech and the Slovak republics include rugged mountains and rich farmland. The River Danube flows along the Czech border and through the plains of central Hungary.

Central Europe has warm summers but cold, snowy winters. Industries include machinery, cars, mining, and the making of beers, wines, and jams. More and more tourists come to visit beautiful old cities such as Krakow, Prague, and Budapest.

Lithuania, like Poland, is a strongly Roman Catholic country. Latvia and Estonia are largely Protestant.

RUSSIA

Gulf of Finland

Tallinn

ESTONIA

Gulf of Riga

Riga

LATVIA

LITHUANIA

Vilnius

BELARUS

Kaliningrad (RUSSIA)

Gdansk

POLAND

Warsaw

Vistula

Lodz

Poznan

Shoppers buy vegetables from a **market stall** in Prague. Central European farms produce wheat, potatoes, barley, corn, sugarbeet and sunflowers.

GERMANY

Vístula

Wroclaw

Krakow

Prague

CZECH REPUBLIC

AUSTRIA

Bratislava

SLOVAK REPUBLIC

ROMANIA

Budapest

HUNGARY

More than 1,000 years ago, **Wenceslas** ruled Bohemia, which is now part of the Czech Republic. His statue may be seen in Prague. He is remembered in the words of a Christmas carol, *Good King Wenceslas*.

This fine old **tall ship** is from Poland. It is used for training young sailors. The Baltic Sea has been a center of trade for thousands of years.

These women are wearing **Estonian costume**. Estonia has been ruled by many other countries over the ages, but has managed to keep up its old traditions.

Goulash is a dish that was first made in Hungary. It is a beef stew flavored with spicy red pepper and sour cream.

Europe

The son of an Albanian farmer shows off his favorite cow. **Albania** is a small, mountainous country on the Adriatic coast.

It is time to make hay on this **Romanian farm**. Everyone in the family lends a hand. The hay will be fed to the animals during the cold months of winter.

The **Parthenon** is a splendid temple, built in the days of the ancient Greeks. It still towers over Athens, the capital city of Greece.

UKRAINE

Ljubljana
SLOVENIA

Zagreb
CROATIA

Kupa

Sava

Drava

HUNGARY

Tisz

Timisoara

Osijek

VOJVODINA

Belgrade

Smederevo

BOSNIA - HERZEGOVINA

Sarajevo

DINARIC

Split

YUGOSLAVIA

SERBIA

MONTENEGRO

Dubrovnik   Podgorica   KOSOVO

Lake Scutari

Skopje

MACEDONIA

Tiranë

ALBANIA

Corfu

GREECE

Mt Olympus
9,567 ft

Cluj-Napoca

Tîrgu Mures

ROMANIA

Alba Iulia

Brasov

Moldoveanu
8,341 ft

TRANSYLVANIAN ALPS

Bucharest

BALKAN MOUNTAINS

Kamch

Sofia

Kazanluk

BULGARIA

Stara Zagora

Plovdiv

Thessaloníki

Iasi

Lesbos

AEGEAN
SEA

Chios

Ándros

Sámo

Athens

Náxo

Thíra

Cythera

SEA OF CRE

Iráklion

Crete

Romania and the Balkans

Romania lies on the Black Sea coast. It is a land of mountains and forests. A large triangle of land stretches southward from Central Europe, ending in chains of islands. It is called the Balkan peninsula and is bordered by the Adriatic, Black, and Aegean Seas. The region has rocky mountain ranges and often suffers from earthquakes. Summers are dry and hot. Winters are very cold in the north, but mild in the south. The region produces timber, wines, olives, fruit, and dairy products.

Bulgaria lies in the northeast of the peninsula. It has large areas of rich farmland. The northwestern Balkan lands used to be part of one big nation called Yugoslavia, but they now make up five different countries. Greece is the southernmost country of the Balkans and includes many islands. Its ancient villages and fine beaches attract many tourists.

MOLDOVA
Galati
MOUTHS OF THE DANUBE
OBRUJA
Constanta
Varna
BLACK SEA

Roses are picked in the Kazanluk region of **Bulgaria**. Their sweet-smelling petals are used to make attar of roses, an oil used in making perfumes.

Churches, whitewashed villages, and blue seas are typical of the Greek lands. This is **Thira**, a volcanic island that is also known as Santorini.

Greek meals might include salad with olives, seafood such as fish or squid, stuffed peppers, beans, a type of wine called retsina, and sweet, sticky pastries such as baklava.

Cos

Rhodes

Zagreb, the capital of **Croatia**, is near the Slovenian border, on the Sava River. The city is on the main route from western Europe to Greece.

Sunflowers are grown as a crop in many parts of the Balkans. Their seeds may be pressed to make vegetable oil or roasted for eating.

25

Russian Federation

The Russian Federation is the world's biggest country. It stretches across two continents, Europe and Asia. When the sun is rising in Vladivostok, on the Pacific Coast, it is setting on the capital, Moscow. In the Arctic north there is an icy plain, the tundra. To the south of this there are huge forests, the home of brown bears. The countryside also takes in rolling farmland called steppes, deserts, and high mountain ranges. Europe's longest river is the Volga, more than 2,300 miles long, which flows into the Caspian Sea. To the east is Baikal, the deepest lake in the world.

Before 1991 all the countries on this map were part of one huge country called the Soviet Union. After 1991 many of the lands around the Soviet borders broke away to form separate countries. More than a hundred different peoples live in the region, beside the Russians themselves.

St. Basil's Cathedral stands in Red Square, in Moscow.

In the days of the Soviet Union, big statues were put up showing people working hard for their country. These **farmers** are harvesting wheat. It is still an important crop today.

FINLAND
BARENT SEA
Murmansk
Archangel
St Petersburg
BELARUS
Minsk
Moscow
UKRAINE
Kiev
Nizhniy Novgorod
Kazan
Chisinau
MOLDOVA
Don
Volga
Samara
Yekaterinb
Ural
URAL MOUNTAIN
BLACK SEA
GEORGIA
ARMENIA
AZERBAIJAN
Caspian Sea
KAZAKHSTAN
Aqm
Aral Sea
TURKMENISTAN
Bishkel
Ashgabat
Tashkent
IRAN
Dushanb
TAJIKISTA

One third of **Armenians** still work on the land. They produce vegetables and fruit or raise sheep and cattle.

Fine **silk** is produced and woven into cloth in the Imeretia region of Georgia.

In the Middle Ages, Russian monks made beautiful **Bibles** like this one, and painted holy pictures called icons.

Wrangel I.

KAMCHATKA PENINSULA

Franz Josef Land

Severnaya Zemlya

New Siberian Islands

Novaya Zemlya

KARA SEA

EAST SIBERIAN UPLANDS

CENTRAL SIBERIAN PLATEAU

Yenisey

Lena

Yakutsk

SEA OF OKHOTSK

Sakhalin

RUSSIA

Ob

Angara

Amur

Khabarovsk

Sour cream

Omsk

Novosibirsk

Irkutsk

Lake Baykal

CHINA

Vladivostok

Blinis

Beetroot

CHINA

Almaty

KYRGYZSTAN

Borscht is made from beetroots and served with sour cream and blinis.

Canada and Greenland

ARCTIC OCEAN

Most Canadian towns are in the south, near the United States border, the Great Lakes, or the St. Lawrence River. The north is a wilderness, with frozen plains, vast forests, mountains, and blue lakes. Winters are long and severe, but summers can be mild or warm. Most Canadians are English-speaking, descended from British settlers. A large number are French-speaking, especially in the province of Québec. There are also First Peoples, such as the Innu, Mohawk, Cree, and Micmac. In Arctic Canada are the Inuit people, who traditionally live by hunting seals and polar bears.

Inuit people also live in Greenland, along with descendants of Danish settlers. This is the world's largest island. Its rocky land is covered in a thick sheet of Arctic ice.

Banks Island

BEAUFORT SEA

Victoria Island

ALASKA (U.S.A.)

MACKENZIE

Mackenzie

Liard

Norman Wells

Great Bear Lake

YUKON TERRITORY

Whitehorse

NORTHWEST TERRITORIES

Great Slave Lake

R O C K Y

BRITISH COLUMBIA

QUEEN CHARLOTTE ISLANDS

ALBERTA

CAN

MANITOBA

SASKATCHEWAN

Calgary

Vancouver Island

Vancouver

Regina

Winnipeg

UNITED STATES OF AMERIC

Maple trees grow colorful leaves in autumn. The maple leaf is a badge of Canada and is shown on the national flag.

Totem poles are still raised outside villages by the First Peoples of British Columbia. They are carved with birds and beasts and figures from myths, legends and family history.

*Ellesmere
Island*

BAFFIN BAY

Baffin Island

**GREENLAND
(Denmark)**

The Niagara Falls lie on the border between Ontario, Canada, and the state of New York. The power of the falling water is used to make electricity.

LABRADOR
SEA

Parts of the **St. Lawrence** river have been turned into a "seaway" or canal. This allows ships to reach Lake Ontario from the Atlantic Ocean.

HUDSON BAY

ADA

NEWFOUNDLAND

St John's

ONTARIO

QUEBEC

PRINCE
EDWARD
ISLAND

St. Lawrence

NEW
BRUNSWICK

NOVA SCOTIA

Quebec

Lake Superior

Ottawa

Montreal

Lake Huron

Toronto

Lake Ontario

Niagara Falls
*Lake
Erie*

Officers of the Royal Canadian Mounted Police are known as **"Mounties."** On parade, they wear smart red jackets and big hats.

The United States of America

The North American **raccoon** is a furry little creature with black patches on its eyes and a ringed tail. It comes out by night.

The United States of America (USA) stretch the whole way from the Atlantic Ocean to the Pacific. There are 50 states in all. They take in woodlands, whose leaves turn red and gold each autumn, and long ranges of hills such as the Appalachians. They include the Great Lakes and the rivers Mississippi and Missouri, which flow into the steamy Gulf of Mexico. There are wide open grasslands called prairies, which are given over to farming and cattle ranching. There is the great Rocky Mountain chain. There are the burning dry deserts of the southwest and the rainy, misty forests of Oregon and Washington State. Two American states are separated from the others. They are Alaska, stretching from Canada into the frozen Arctic, and Hawaii, a group of islands and volcanoes far out in the Pacific Ocean.

CANADA

Seattle
WASHINGTON

CASCADE RANGE

OREGON

IDAHO

MONTANA

Snake

WYOMING

Black Hills

Rapid C

Great Salt Lake

Rock Springs

Boulder

NEVADA

UTAH

Denver

San Francisco

GREAT BASIN

Grand Junction

COLORADO

Las Vegas

CALIFORNIA

Grand Canyon

NEW MEXICO

Los Angeles

ARIZONA

Colorado

San Diego

Phoenix

Rio Grande

Douglas

MEXICO

Rainbow Bridge is an arch of pink rock in the state of Utah. Over the ages, wind and water have worn it down into this strange shape.

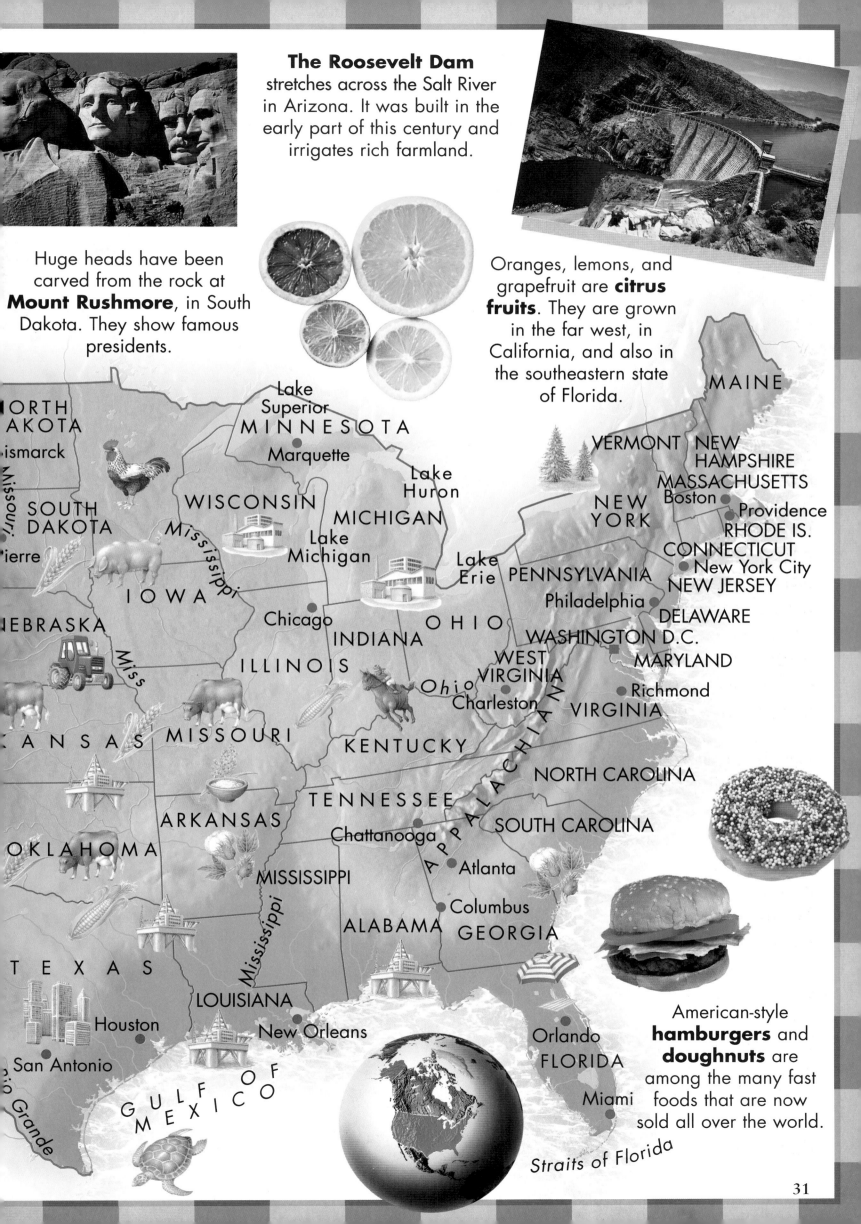

The Roosevelt Dam stretches across the Salt River in Arizona. It was built in the early part of this century and irrigates rich farmland.

Huge heads have been carved from the rock at **Mount Rushmore**, in South Dakota. They show famous presidents.

Oranges, lemons, and grapefruit are **citrus fruits**. They are grown in the far west, in California, and also in the southeastern state of Florida.

American-style **hamburgers** and **doughnuts** are among the many fast foods that are now sold all over the world.

NORTH DAKOTA
Bismarck

Missouri

Lake Superior

MINNESOTA
Marquette

Lake Huron

WISCONSIN

MICHIGAN
Lake Michigan

Lake Erie

MAINE

VERMONT NEW HAMPSHIRE
MASSACHUSETTS
Boston
Providence

NEW YORK

RHODE IS.
CONNECTICUT
New York City
NEW JERSEY

SOUTH DAKOTA
Pierre

Mississippi

IOWA

Chicago

OHIO

INDIANA

PENNSYLVANIA
Philadelphia

DELAWARE

WASHINGTON D.C.
MARYLAND

NEBRASKA

Miss

ILLINOIS

Ohio

WEST VIRGINIA
Charleston

Richmond

VIRGINIA

KANSAS

MISSOURI

KENTUCKY

NORTH CAROLINA

ARKANSAS

TENNESSEE

SOUTH CAROLINA

OKLAHOMA

Chattanooga

Atlanta

MISSISSIPPI

Mississippi

ALABAMA

Columbus

GEORGIA

TEXAS

LOUISIANA

Houston

New Orleans

Orlando
FLORIDA

San Antonio

Rio Grande

GULF OF MEXICO

Miami

Straits of Florida

31

The USA has many big, bustling cities. In the west is San Francisco. It is a beautiful port beside the blue Pacific Ocean. Los Angeles is a huge city full of traffic. A part of it, called Hollywood, is where many famous films have been made. Chicago, on Lake Michigan, was where skyscrapers were first built, more than a hundred years ago. Detroit, on Lake Erie, is where many automobiles are made. And New York City, in the east, is the biggest city of them all. It is nicknamed the Big Apple. The capital of the country is Washington D.C. This is the center of government and is also where the US president lives, in the White House. It isn't in one of the states but in a special district called Columbia.

Many different peoples live in the USA today. Native Americans are descended from the very first people to settle in North America. They include peoples such as the Navajo, Apache, and Cree. Many Americans are descended from European settlers. New

The **World Trade Center** has two tall towers. They rise up from the water's edge on the island of Manhattan. This is right at the center of New York City, one of the largest and busiest cities in the world.

Rattlesnakes live in the hot, dry lands of Texas and the southwest. They are very dangerous. They rattle their tails as a warning before they bite you.

Dance and song make up a **traditional welcome** to the Hawaiian islands. Hawaii's links with the USA go back 100 years.

The USA has many exciting **theme parks**, where children can enjoy fun and fantasy.

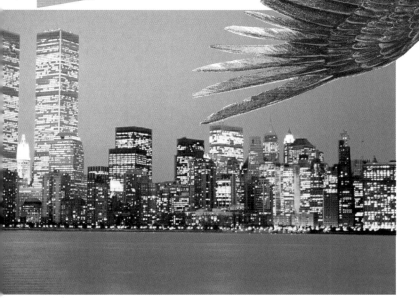

The **Californian condor** is very, very rare. It has huge wings, about 10 feet across.

other languages such as Spanish are spoken in some cities. The USA is a country with rich farmland and many mineral mines. Its factories produce computers, cars, drinks and foods, clothing, and all sorts of other goods. It is also a center of the film industry, banking, and business. This has made it one of the world's richest and most powerful countries.

settlers came from Britain and Ireland, Italy, France, Spain, Greece, Germany, Poland, and the Netherlands. African Americans are the descendants of West Africans who were brought to America hundreds of years ago. Some Americans originally came from Asia, including Jews, Chinese, and Vietnamese. The Hawaiians are Polynesians, one of the Pacific peoples. All these different groups are proud of their background, but they now belong to one big country, the USA. Today most Americans speak English, but

A shuttle is launched into space on the back of huge rockets. It is leaving Cape Canaveral in Florida.

The bright city lights of **Las Vegas** shine out over the desert in the state of Nevada. People come here to gamble, see shows, and stay in hotels.

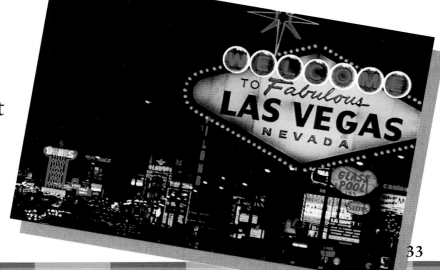

Mexico, Central America, and the Caribbean

Mexico lies between the Gulf of Mexico and the Pacific Ocean. It is a land of hot deserts, mountain ranges, forests, and sandy beaches. Earthquakes are common and there are volcanoes, too. Mexico City is the country's capital. Once it was the chief city of the Aztec people and called Tenochtitlán. Many great civilizations were started in the region long ago.

To the south of Mexico are the seven small countries of Central America. Panama is crossed by a canal, which links the Atlantic and Pacific Oceans. Spanish is the main language of the region. Many of its

Guacamole

Chillies

Tortillas are cornmeal pancakes made in Central America. They may be served with beans and hot chillies.

Tortillas

Beer

Baja California

SIERRA MADRE

Rio Grande

SIERRA MADRE

Culiacán

Matamoros

Monterrey

Guadalajara

León

Mexico City

Veracruz

MEXICO

Coatzacoalcas

Acapulco

PACIFIC OCEAN

GULF OF MEXICO

Cancún

Havana

CUB

Cayman Islands (U.K

Belmopan

BELIZE

GUATEMALA   **HONDURAS**

Guatemala City   Tegucigalpa

San Salvador

EL SALVADOR

NICARAGUA

Managua

San José   Panam

COSTA RICA

PANAM

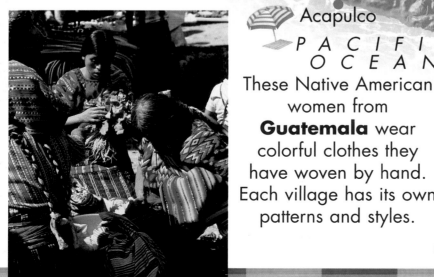

These Native American women from **Guatemala** wear colorful clothes they have woven by hand. Each village has its own patterns and styles.

peoples are descended from the Spanish soldiers who invaded the Americas nearly 500 years ago. Others are descended from Native Americans. Central American crops include corn and bananas.

The Caribbean Sea lies to the east of Central America. It has thousands of islands, the largest of which is Cuba. Caribbean peoples include many whose ancestors came from West Africa. There are also some Caribbeans of Native American, Spanish, French, British, Dutch, and Asian descent. The islands have a warm, tropical climate in which sugarcane and bananas grow well. Hurricanes are common in the later summer and autumn. The islands are famous for their carnivals.

Brilliantly colored **hummingbirds** hover as they sip nectar from flowers. They are found in both Central America and the Caribbean.

Warm blue seas, fine beaches, and watersports attract millions of tourists to the Caribbean islands each year. This is **Barbados**.

How would you like to dive off this cliff into the sea? This is one of the sights to be seen at **Acapulco**, in Mexico.

AHAMAS

Turks & Caicos Islands (U.K.)

Virgin Is. (U.K. & U.S.)

ANTIGUA & BARBUDA

Puerto Rico (U.S.)

ST. KITTS & NEVIS

Montserrat (U.K.)

Guadeloupe (FR.)

DOMINICA

Martinique (FR.)

HAITI

DOMINICAN REPUBLIC

JAMAICA

ST. LUCIA

CARIBBEAN SEA

ST. VINCENT & THE GRENADINES

BARBADOS

GRENADA

TRINIDAD & TOBAGO

Mexico and parts of Central America have many ancient ruins and statues, like this **warrior** carved from stone. They date back to the ancient civilizations that once grew up here.

Old churches and buildings, like this one in **Costa Rica**, remind us that this region was once ruled by Spain.

The Northern Andes

South America is joined to Central America by a narrow strip of land. To the south, the Andes mountains run all the way down the continent. Their high, snowy peaks divide the hot lands along the coast from the rain forests and great rivers of the east. Colombia is a beautiful country, which lies across three bands of the Andes range. The rocks are mined for gold and precious green stones called emeralds. Ecuador is named for the Spanish word for Equator. Bananas and sugarcane grow in the warm climate here, and coffee too on the slopes of hills. In Peru, farmers work high in the mountains, growing potatoes, corn and a grain called quinoa. Along the coast fishermen catch tuna and sardines. Bolivia has great forests and tin mines.

About 500 years ago, the Inca people ruled a huge empire in the Andes. It was conquered by Spanish soldiers. Many peoples of the region are descended from Native American peoples and from the Spanish.

This boat is made of reeds, by the **Aymara people.** They live around Lake Titicaca, which is on the border between Peru and Bolivia.

The green turtle lives in the sea along the coasts of Peru, Ecuador, and Colombia. It breeds on lonely, sandy beaches and is becoming very rare.

VENEZUELA

PANAMA

CARIBBEAN SEA

COLOMBIA

● Bogotá

ECUADOR

Quito

Amazon

Iquitos ●

S

E

BOLIVIA

Sucre

La Paz

Lake Poopó

PERU

Lake Titicaca

PARAGUAY

CHILE

Lima

Nazca

Ucayali

PACIFIC OCEAN

Andean musicians play the rondador or pan pipes, rattles called maracas, guitars, and drums.

maracas

This peak towers above the rocks of the **Andes**. It is covered in snow, even though it is near the Equator, in Ecuador. It is called Cotopaxi and is the world's highest active volcano.

pan pipes

Llamas live high in the Andes. They carry baggage along high, narrow mountain paths. Their wool is used for weaving into cloth.

This mother and baby belong to the **Quechua people**. They live near the old Inca capital of Cuzco, in Peru. Most Quechua live in mountain villages and work as farmers. They grow potatoes and corn, and raise sheep and llamas.

The ancient peoples of Colombia made many beautiful things from **gold** and precious stones. They used knives like these for their religious ceremonies.

37

Brazil and its Neighbors

Brazil is the biggest country in South America. It is a hot country with grassland, swamps, and dry bush. A large area is covered in rain forest. This is the home of monkeys, brightly colored parrots, and gigantic snakes called anacondas. One of the world's two longest rivers, the Amazon, flows through the forest to the Atlantic Ocean. On the coast there are many big cities. Some city dwellers are rich, but many are very poor.

Venezuela is on the Caribbean coast. It is crossed by another great river called the Orinoco.

A large sea inlet called Lake Maracaibo is the center of Venezuela's oil industry. Three other small countries, called Guyana, Suriname, and French Guiana, lie on the tropical north coast. They produce sugarcane, rice, chilli peppers, and fruits.

This part of South America is home to many different Native American peoples, as well as people descended from Africans and Europeans. The region was once ruled by Portugal, Spain, France, Britain, and the Netherlands.

Caracas

VENEZUELA
Orinoco

COLOMBIA

PERU

The **Iguaçu Falls** lie on the border between Brazil and Argentina. The river thunders over hundreds of waterfalls.

This cathedral is in **Brasília**, the capital of Brazil. This modern city was specially built inland, to the south of the great forests.

There are many different kinds of **poison-arrow frog** in South America. Their deadly poison is smeared on arrows and darts by Native American hunters.

This beautiful tropical plant is called the **bird-of-paradise flower**.

TRINIDAD & TOBAGO

Angel Falls

Georgetown

GUYANA

Paramaribo

Cayenne

SURINAM

FRENCH GUIANA

G U I A N A

Negro

Manaus

Amazon

Santarém

BRAZIL

Guaporé

BOLIVIA

Teresina

Fortaleza

Salvador

Brasília

Paraná

Belo Horizonte

São Paulo

Rio de Janeiro

ARGENTINA

Uruguay

URUGUAY

In the southeast of **Venezuela** there are sheer, flat-topped mountains called tepuis. They rise from beautiful lakes and green tropical forests.

Many tropical trees grow in Brazil. One produces seeds called **brazil nuts**. They make delicious snacks.

The **puma** is a big, fierce cat. In North America it is called the cougar or mountain lion.

A big **statue of Jesus** looks out over the city of Rio de Janeiro, in Brazil. It is on a high mountain called the Sugarloaf.

39

Argentina and its Neighbors

Southern South America is a big triangle of land. The pointed end stretches south toward Antarctica. It breaks up into islands around Tierra del Fuego. Gales whip up huge waves around the southern tip, which is called Cape Horn. As you travel north, you come to the dry, windy valleys of Patagonia, the high Andes mountains, the rich grassland of the Pampas, and the hot, damp Gran Chaco region.

Argentina is a big country, which raises beef cattle and sheep. It borders the Atlantic Ocean. Far offshore are the remote Falkland or Malvinas islands. Uruguay and Paraguay are two small countries to the north, which also raise cattle. Chile, to the west of the Andes, is a long, narrow land. It borders the Pacific Ocean. It has large areas of desert, where it hardly ever rains. It also has warm farmland, where grapes can be grown.

PARAGUAY

Concepción • **Asunción**

GRAN CHACO

Pilcomayo

Bermejo

Formosa

Corrientes

Paraguay

Paraná

Neg?o

URUGUAY

Montevideo

Córdoba •

Rosario •

Buenos Aires

P A M P A S

ARGENTINA

Santiago •

CHILE

Concepción •

ATACAMA DESERT

The snow-capped volcano of **Villarrica** rises above a milder landscape near Pucón, in Chile.

Tomatoes were first grown in South America, on the slopes of the Andes mountains. Today they are grown all over the world.

FALKLAND/MALVINAS ISLANDS

● Stanley

Monti

P A T A G

PACIFIC OCEAN

Tierra del Fuego

Cape Horn

The **rhea** is a large South American bird that can grow to 5 feet tall. It cannot fly and lives on the Pampas.

The **gauchos** are the cowboys of the Pampas grasslands in Argentina. They are skilled at riding horses and roping cattle. They used to be famous for their wild adventures.

PASAJE
PREFECTO LUIS PEDRO FIQUE

Ushuaia is a port in **Tierra del Fuego**, in the far south of Argentina. The people who live there raise sheep and go fishing.

BLACK SEA

Istanbul

Ankara

TURKEY

Mt. Ararat
Lake Van 17,007 ft

CASPIAN SEA

Mt. Damavand
18,380 ft ▲

Tehran

Nicosia

CYPRUS

LEBANON

SYRIA

Euphrates

Tigris

Beirut Damascus

ISRAEL

Amman

Jerusalem

JORDAN

Baghdad

IRAQ

Esfahan

KUWAIT
Kuwait

The Gulf

BAHRAIN

QATAR
Doha

These delicious greenish colored nuts are grown in western Turkey.
Pistachios make a tasty snack and are also used to flavor ice cream.

Long ago the ancient Greeks lived in what is now western Turkey. The city of **Ephesus**, site of a temple to the goddess Artemis, later became an early center of Christianity.

Medina

Riyadh

SAUDI ARABIA

Jiddah
Mecca

Rub' al Khali
(Empty Quarter)

This girl is from San'a, the **Yemeni** capital. She is a Moslem and so wears a veil over her face. Judaism, Christianity, and Islam all started in Southwest Asia.

San'a

YEMEN

Gulf of Aden

Aden

DJIBOUTI

Southwest Asia

This region of Asia is often called the Near East or the Middle East. Its western parts border the Mediterranean Sea. These have a gentle, warm climate, which makes it possible to grow fruits such as oranges and lemons. The Arabian peninsula is the land surrounded by the Red Sea, the Indian Ocean, and the Persian Gulf. It is occupied by Jordan, Saudi Arabia, and the small countries of Yemen, Oman, United Arab Emirates (UAE), Qatar, Bahrain, and Kuwait. This a land of hot, sandy deserts. Little can grow here, but it is rich in oil and natural gas.

Eastern Syria and Iraq are also desert regions, but these are crossed by the rivers Tigris and Euphrates. It was here that the world's first farmers founded towns and cities thousands of years ago. Eastern Turkey and northern Iran include mountains, windswept plains and rolling grasslands, which are very cold in winter. Iran also has ranges of mountains and deserts.

Mashhad

IRAN

Abu Dhabi

Gulf of Oman

NITED ARAB EMIRATES ■ Muscat

OMAN

Socotra (YEMEN)

These towers in **Kuwait** are used to take the salt out of seawater, so that it can be drunk or used on the land.

Beautiful **pearls** form in oysters in the warm seas of Southwest Asia. They are very valuable.

This camel rider is one of the **Bedouin**, a nomadic people of the region. Camels are the ideal transport for desert areas.

India and its Neighbors

This mass of land is so big that it is sometimes called the Indian subcontinent, or simply the subcontinent. It is separated from Central Asia by the world's biggest mountains, which are in the Himalaya and Karakoram ranges. These climb to 29,028 feet above sea level at Mount Everest. Snowy peaks stretch all the way from eastern Afghanistan, through northern Pakistan and India to Nepal and Bhutan.

To the south are the wide, dusty plains of India, crossed by the Ganges. In Bangladesh, this river splits into many channels before flowing into the Bay of Bengal. India is a country of deserts, forested hills, small villages, and large bustling cities. The climate is mostly tropical and very hot, with monsoon winds bringing heavy summer rainstorms. In the far south is the tropical island nation of Sri Lanka.

The region produces wheat, tea, sugarcane, rice, jute, and cotton. It includes the sites of ancient civilizations and places which are holy to Hindus, Buddhists, Sikhs, and Muslims.

Mount Everest is the highest mountain on Earth. It lies on the border between Nepal and Tibet, in the Himalaya range.

Colorful, sparkling costumes are worn by these **Indian dancers.** India is famous for its richly colored silks and cottons and its silver jewelry.

Kabul

Khyber Pass

Islamabad

Lahore

PAKISTAN

Indus

NEPAL

Delhi ▪**New Delhi**

HIMALAYAS

Coriander

Ground turmeric

Ginger

Andaman & Nicobar Is. (India)

Indian food includes delicious curries, chutneys, rice, and vegetable dishes. They are cooked with different **kinds of spice.**

Brahmaputra

Dhaka

Varanasi

Ganges

Kanpur

Calcutta

INDIA

BAY OF BENGAL

This **Bengal tiger** has become very rare. It is protected in special reserves in India, Bangladesh, and Nepal.

Nagpur

Godavari

Hyderabad

Chennai (Madras)

Bangalore

SRI LANKA

Colombo

Galle

Ahmadabad

Surat

Mumbai (Bombay)

Pune

ARABIAN SEA

INDIAN OCEAN

A woman picks **tea** in the green hills of Sri Lanka. This small island nation to the south of India is the biggest exporter of tea in the world.

MALDIVES

Many people say that the **Taj Mahal,** a marble tomb, is the most beautiful building in the world. It was built near Agra in India by a Muslim emperor named Shah Jahan, who ruled from 1627 to 1666.

China and its Neighbors

China covers an area about the size of western Europe. It is ringed by high mountains, empty deserts, and tropical seas where fierce storms called typhoons are common.

Most people live in the fertile eastern part of the country, which is crossed by great rivers such as the Huang He and the Chang Jiang. More people live in China than in any other country in the world. Chinese farmers grow rice, tea, wheat, and corn. China is the center of a very ancient civilization and was famous in history for its pottery and fine silk.

The Mongols live in a northern part of China and also in the rolling grasslands and deserts of Mongolia itself. The Koreans live to the northeast, on a peninsula containing North and South Korea.

KAZAKHSTAN

MONGOLIA

Ürümqi

TAKLIMAKAN DESERT

CHINA

PLATEAU OF TIBET

INDIA

HIMALAYA

Lhasa

Salw

Mt. Everest▲ 29,029 ft

Qin Shi Huangdi was the first emperor of China. When he died in 210BC his tomb was surrounded by a **buried army**. This was made up of thousands of life-sized soldiers, made of clay.

Traditional wooden sailing boats called **junks** may still be seen among the more modern ships around the coasts of China.

There are many different styles of Chinese cooking, from Beijing in the north to Guangzhou in the south. Rice, noodles, and dumplings are popular, steamed in **bamboo containers**.

Many **Mongols** follow their herds of sheep on horseback. They live in a round felt tent known as a **ger** or **yurt**.

Amur

RUSSIA

Harbin

Ulan Bator

Shenyang

NORTH KOREA

P'yongyang

Hong Kong is a small, crowded piece of land in southern China. It was mostly ruled by Britain from 1842 until 1997. It is a center of business and tourism.

GOBI DESERT

Dalian

Seoul

SOUTH KOREA

Beijing

Tianjin

Zibo

YELLOW SEA

Taiyuan

EAST CHINA SEA

Huang He

Lanzhou

ang He

Xi'an

Nanjing

Shanghai

Chengdu

Wuhan

Chongqing

Fuzhou

Taipei

TAIWAN

Farm workers in China plant out **rice** seedlings in a flooded paddy. China has so many people to feed that every possible bit of spare land is used to grow crops. Rice is served with most meals.

Kunming

Guangzhou

Hong Kong

MACAO

Mekong

Hainan

47

Asia
Japan

Thousands of small islands lie to the east of China on the edge of the Pacific Ocean. They make up a country called Japan. There are four main islands—Hokkaido, Honshu, Shikoku, and Kyushu. These are mostly very mountainous, so the big cities have spread along the strips of flat land around the coast. This is where most of the good farmland is sited, too. Japan produces rice and tea, and has a large fishing fleet. The north of the country is cold and snowy in winter, but the south has a warm, tropical climate.

Japan has very few resources such as oil or coal. Even so, it is a very modern country which has many big businesses and produces cars and electrical goods. At the same time Japan is an ancient country, with many traditional customs and ceremonies. You can still see beautiful Buddhist temples and castles too, dating back to the Middle Ages. Japan has long been famous for its beautiful art, architecture, and pottery. Japanese artists carry on these traditions in modern dance, films, and even in computer games.

The Japanese capital is **Tokyo**. It is a center of business and industry and merges with another great city, the port of Yokohama. It has suffered in the past from severe earthquakes.

The high-speed **Bullet Train** has become a symbol of modern Japan. Japan's islands are linked by some of the world's longest and most modern bridges and tunnels.

HOKKAIDO

Asahi Mt. 7,511 ft

Sapporo

Kuril Is. (Russia)

Kitaka

JAPAN

The slopes of **Mount Fuji** are covered in snow. Japanese artists have painted this beautiful volcano many times.

Traditional dress is still worn in Japan on many special occasions. This woman wears sandals and a silk gown called a kimono.

Sumo wrestlers weigh in at about 300 pounds. Their aim is to topple their opponent or throw them out of the ring. The match starts with long ceremonies, but the action is normally over very quickly.

Favorite Japanese foods include rice, fish, prawns, seaweed, pork, bean curd, and noodles. These are traditionally eaten with chopsticks.

Sendai

Mito

Yokohama

Tokyo

HONSHU

Mt. Fuji 12,385 ft

PACIFIC OCEAN

Nagoya

Kyoto

Kobe
Osaka

Kii Channel

SHIKOKU

Hiroshima

Kitakyushu

Fukuoka

KYUSHU

Southeast Asia

The southeast of the Asian continent borders India and China. It is a land of flooded ricefields, forests, remote hill country, and great rivers, such as the Irrawaddy and the Mekong. This region has beautiful Buddhist temples and ruins left behind by ancient civilizations. Sadly, it has also seen terrible wars in the last 50 years, while in some areas the traditional way of life has been completely changed by tourism or, in the cities of Singapore or Kuala Lumpur, by big business.

The mainland states include Myanmar, Thailand, Cambodia, Laos, and Vietnam. Malaysia takes up part of the mainland but also most of the forested, tropical island of Borneo. The small state of Brunei is in the north of Borneo. The south of the region is occupied by the long chains of islands which make up Indonesia. In the far east, bordering the Pacific Ocean, are the Philippines.

People of both Indian and Chinese descent live in the city of **Singapore** and their styles of cooking have mingled—deliciously!

This ornate stone demon guards the royal palace in **Bangkok**, capital of Thailand.

The **orangutan** lives in the rain forests of Borneo and Sumatra. Throughout Southeast Asia forests are threatened by logging, clearance, and fires.

A boat is anchored by the banks of the Hue river, in northeastern **Vietnam**. Cone-shaped straw hats protect the wearer from tropical sun and monsoon rains.

While most Indonesians are Muslims, the **Balinese** are Hindus. The island of Bali has many beautiful old temples and palaces, where dances like this can be seen.

IETNAM

Luzon

■ Manila

PHILIPPINES

SULU SEA

Mindanao

Bandar Seri Begawan

S I A **BRUNEI**

CELEBES SEA

BORNEO

Sulawesi

Moluccas

I N D O N E S I A

NEW GUINEA

BANDA SEA

A V A *SEA*

FLORES SEA

va

■ Surabaya

Lombok

Bali

Sumba

Timor

Singapore is a tiny independent country. Most of it is taken up by the city of Singapore, an international center of business and trade.

Meet the **komodo dragon**, the world's biggest lizard. It lives only on Komodo and a few neighboring islands in Indonesia.

North and West Africa

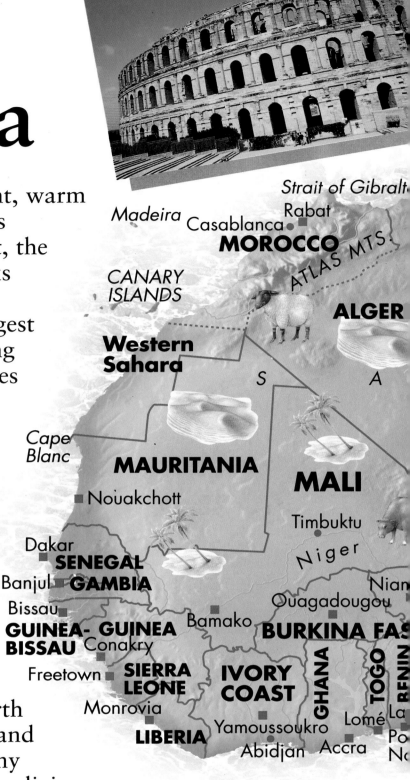

The Mediterranean coast has a pleasant, warm climate. To the south, beyond the Atlas mountains, is the world's largest desert, the Sahara. Its burning hot sands and rocks stretch all the way from Mauritania to Egypt. The River Nile, the world's longest river, meets the sea in Egypt after a long journey northward across Sudan. It rises in the mountains of Central Africa and Ethiopia.

The countries bordering the southern edge of the Sahara make up the Sahel. This is a dry, dusty region where thin grass is grazed by cattle and goats. Nearer the coast, on the Gulf of Guinea, there is fertile farmland, forest and the oil-rich lands around the River Niger. West Africa produces peanuts, cocoa, palm oil, and cotton.

Peoples of the north include Berbers and Arabs. The many different peoples living to the south of the Sahara are mostly Black Africans. Religions of the region include Islam, Christianity, and spirit religions.

This grumpy-looking camel is looking out over the **Pyramids**, the royal burial sites of ancient Egypt. Africa's first great civilization grew up in Egypt about 5,000 years ago.

Tutankhamun died in 1327BC. He was ruler, or pharaoh, of ancient Egypt and was buried with all sorts of rich treasures.

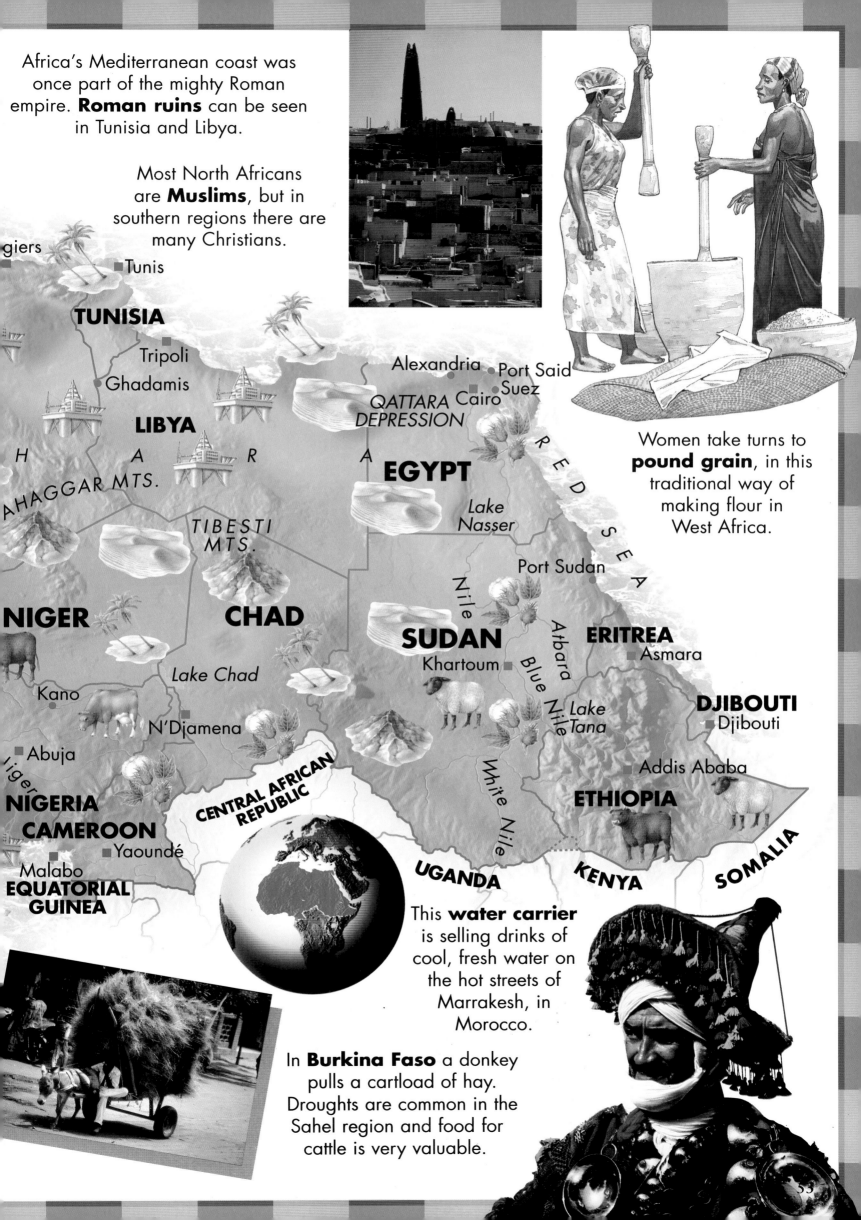

Africa's Mediterranean coast was once part of the mighty Roman empire. **Roman ruins** can be seen in Tunisia and Libya.

Most North Africans are **Muslims**, but in southern regions there are many Christians.

giers

Tunis

TUNISIA

Tripoli

Ghadamis

LIBYA

Alexandria   Port Said
Suez

QATTARA Cairo
DEPRESSION

EGYPT

*Lake
Nasser*

H   A   R

AHAGGAR MTS.

*TIBESTI
MTS.*

NIGER

CHAD

Kano

Lake Chad

N'Djamena

Abuja

iger

NIGERIA

CAMEROON

Yaoundé

Malabo

**EQUATORIAL
GUINEA**

**CENTRAL AFRICAN
REPUBLIC**

Nile

Port Sudan

SUDAN

Khartoum

Atbara

Blue Nile

ERITREA

Asmara

DJIBOUTI

Djibouti

*Lake
Tana*

Addis Ababa

ETHIOPIA

White Nile

UGANDA

KENYA

SOMALIA

RED SEA

Women take turns to **pound grain**, in this traditional way of making flour in West Africa.

This **water carrier** is selling drinks of cool, fresh water on the hot streets of Marrakesh, in Morocco.

In **Burkina Faso** a donkey pulls a cartload of hay. Droughts are common in the Sahel region and food for cattle is very valuable.

55

Central, Eastern, and Southern Africa

Central Africa is a land of rain forests, crossed by the River Congo. To the south are the Kalahari and Namib deserts, and the mountains and grasslands of South Africa. The east of the continent is divided by the Great Rift Valley, a network of deep cracks in the Earth's surface. It is fringed by volcanoes and in places has filled with water to form long lakes. East Africa includes rich farmland, which produces tobacco, fruit, and vegetables. There are wide grassy plains dotted with thorny trees, grazed by great herds of wild animals including zebra, giraffe and many types of antelope. The continent is bordered by the Atlantic to the west and by the Indian Ocean to the east. Madgascar is Africa's largest island.

The **Masai people** live in southern Kenya and northern Tanzania. Many of them herd cattle.

Vast herds of wild animals still roam eastern and southern Africa. They include lion, antelope, **elephant,** and rhinoceros.

SÃO TOMÉ & PRÍNCIPE

Libreville

REP. C CONG

GABON

Brazzavil

Kinsha

Cabinda (ANGOLA)

Luanda

A N

Bozo

Windhoe

NAMIB DESERT

Wind shapes the shifiting sands of the **Namib desert** in southwestern Africa. This harsh, dry region borders the Atlantic coast for 800 miles.

Sorghum is a grain crop much like corn which thrives in the hot and dry conditions of Zimbabwe.

Cape To

Cape Good H

The **Zulus** are the largest group of peoples living in South Africa. Many different peoples live in the region, each with their own language and traditions.

The River Zambezi forms **Victoria Falls,** a huge waterfall, between Zambia and Zimbabwe. Its local name is Mose-la-Tunya, the "smoke that thunders".

SOMALIA

CENTRAL AFRICAN REPUBLIC
Bangassou

angui

Congo

Uele

UGANDA

KENYA

Mogadishu

Kampala

RWANDA

Lake Victoria

Nairobi

Kigali

DEMOCRATIC REP. OF CONGO

BURUNDI

Kilimanjaro 19,335 ft

Dodoma

SEYCHELLES

Kananga

Lake Tanganyika

Kasai

Sankuru

TANZANIA

INDIAN OCEAN

Lake Malawi (Nyasa)

COMOROS

LA

MALAWI

Lilongwe

Moçambique

ZAMBIA

Lusaka

Zambezi

Blantyre

Mozambique Channel

Harare

MOZAMBIQUE

NAMIBIA

ZIMBABWE

Limpopo

Antananarivo

MAURITIUS

BOTSWANA

Gaborone

MADAGASCAR

KALAHARI DESERT

Pretoria

Maputo

Mbabane

SWAZILAND

Maseru

SOUTH AFRICA

LESOTHO

This animal is a ring-tailed **lemur**. Lemurs are only found on the island of Madagascar. They live in forest and dry scrub land, where they eat fruit and insects.

Australia

The center of Australia is an empty wilderness of desert, rocks, and scrub. It is bordered by grasslands, tropical forests and creeks. In the east are the mountains of the Great Dividing Range. The chief rivers are the Murray and the Darling, in the southeast. The remote country regions of Australia are known as the "outback." They are grazed by huge herds of sheep and cattle, and in places are worked by mining companies.

Most Australians live in the big cities around the coast, such as Brisbane, Sydney, Melbourne, Adelaide, and Perth. Across Bass Strait is the island of Tasmania, which has a cooler climate.

Today's Australians include the first inhabitants of the land, the Aborigines, as well as the descendants of British people who seized their lands about 200 years ago. There are also many people from other European countries and from Asia.

Sydney Opera House rises from Sydney Harbor like a giant sailing ship.

A **giant clam** lies in the tropical waters of this 1,200 mile-long bank of coral.

GREAT
SAND
DESER

GIBSO
DESER

WESTERN
AUSTRALIA

GREAT
VICTOR
DESER

Perth

Archipelago of the
Recherche

Through the surf **rowers** break white water during a beach contest. Australia is famous for its surf.

The **kookaburra** is a common Australian bird. It has a loud cackling call which gives it the nickname of the laughing jackass.

Surfers' Paradise is one of many resorts built along the eastern coast of Australia. Sunshine and surf attract many visitors.

ARAFURA SEA

Darwin

TIMOR SEA

Gulf of
Carpentaria

CAPE
YORK
PENINSULA

Great Barrier Reef

GREAT DIVIDING RANGE

This **frilled lizard** frightens its enemies with a strange display. Many Australian animals are found nowhere else on Earth.

NORTHERN
TERRITORY

AUSTRALIA

Alice Springs

Uluru (Ayers Rock)
2,843 ft

▲

SIMPSON
DESERT

QUEENSLAND

SOUTH AUSTRALIA

L. Eyre

Brisbane

NULLABOR PLAIN

Darling

NEW SOUTH
WALES

GREAT DIVIDING RANGE

Sydney

Adelaide

Murray

Canberra
AUSTRALIAN
CAPITAL
TERRITORY

VICTORIA

Melbourne

TASMAN
SEA

At a sheep station in the outback, the animals are herded **TASMANIA** into pens for **shearing**. Wool and meat are important Australian exports.

Hobart

New Zealand and the Pacific

If you sail eastward from Australia, you reach a group of islands about 1,000 miles out into the Pacific Ocean. They make up a country called New Zealand. There are two main islands, North and South. They include high mountains and glaciers, hot springs, gushing spouts called geysers, and grassy plains. The Maori people were the first people to settle these islands, followed after the 1800s by Europeans, especially the British. New Zealand raises sheep and exports dairy products, fruit, and meat.

The Pacific is the world's biggest ocean stretching all the way to the Americas. It is dotted with small islands, and these are home to three main groups of people—the Polynesians (who include the Maoris), the Micronesians, and the Melanesians. They live by fishing, growing crops such as coconuts and yams, by mining and by tourism.

Yellow Sea

East China Sea

Philippine Sea

SOUTH CHINA SEA

Northern Mariana Islands (USA)

Guam

Federated States of Micronesia

Celebes Sea

Palau

Papua New Guinea

Solom Islar

Coral Sea

Papua New Guinea is made up of many islands. Some small islands are surrounded by shallow reefs.

The **Kiwi** is a flightless bird which comes out by night to search for insects on the forest floor. It is the national emblem of New Zealand.

This **Karawari woman** from Papua New Guinea has painted her face for a traditional tribal gathering.

This is a market in **Vanuatu,** a Pacific nation made up of 80 islands. They produce cocoa, dried coconut, and bananas.

BERING SEA

*N O R T H
P A C I F I C
O C E A N*

Midway
Island (USA)

Wake Island
(USA)

Hawaii (USA)

Marshall
Islands

Nauru   Kiribati

Tuvalu

Vanuat   Samoa   American
        Fiji   Samoa   French
                                    Polynesia
New   Tonga   Cook Islands
Caledonia   (New
(France)   Zealand)

Giant tortoises live on the Galapagos Islands. In fact the islands' name means "tortoises" in Spanish. These Pacific Islands are governed by the South American country of Ecuador.

South Island, New Zealand, has snowfields, glaciers and **high mountains**. Mount Cook reaches 12,395 feet above sea level.

The brown nut of the **coconut**, with its white center, is found inside a large green fruit. Coconuts are a valuable Pacific island export.

Galapagos
(Ecuador)

Huge stone heads were carved by Polynesian settlers on **Easter Island**, about 1,000 years ago.

Auckland

Hamilton

Waikato

Rotorua

L. Taupo

*Ruapehu
9,830 ft*   Napier

Hastings

Palmerston North

Wellington

NEW ZEALAND

Kaibola canoes are the traditional means of transport of the Pacific Islands. This crew is from Papua New Guinea.

SOUTHERN ALPS

Cook Strait

*Mt.Cook
12,395 ft*   Christchurch

This fine **wooden carving** was placed above the door of a Moari building.

Clutha   Dunedin

Invercargill

Stewart Island

Traditionally, **Maoris** wore cloaks and tattooed their faces. Maoris today retain many customs.

59

Polar Lands

The northern part of the globe is called the Arctic. It takes in the northern parts of North America, Europe and Asia. These are lands of ice and snow and deep-frozen treeless soil, called tundra. They surround the Arctic Ocean, of which large areas are permanently capped in thick ice. At the center of this ice cap is the northernmost point on Earth, the North Pole.

Peoples of the Arctic include the Inuit of Greenland and Canada, the Saami of Scandinavia, and the many peoples from the north of the Russian Federation, such as the Chukchi, Yupigyts, Evenks, and Samoyeds. Some live by hunting and fishing, some by herding reindeer, and some in more recent Arctic industries, such as oil and mining. The Arctic Ocean supports fish, whales, walrus, and seals.

The **Inuit people** live in Canada and Greenland. Traditionally their hunters made overnight camps out of blocks of frozen snow. These were shaped into domes.

BERING SEA

ALASKA (USA)

Mackenzie

New Siberian Islands

Lena

C A N A D A

Victoria Island

ARCTIC OCEAN

North Magnetic Pole

★ North Pole

Yenise

Ellesmere Island

Franz Josef Land

Novaya Zemlya

KARA SEA

Ob

GREENLAND (DENMARK)

Svalbard (Norway)

Murmansk

Archangel

ICELAND

Polar bears hunt seals on the ice.

The **Snowy owl** lives in Arctic regions.

Teams of dogs known as huskies, pull sleds across the snow in Antarctica.

The southernmost point on the globe is called the South Pole. It is surrounded by Antarctica, the coldest and windiest land on Earth. This is a land of mountains and dazzling white icefields, split by deep cracks called crevasses. Large areas of frozen sea surround the land. Massive slabs of ice break off in spring to form icebergs. No people have ever settled in Antarctica, but there are scientific bases. Some countries claim parts of Antarctica and there may be rich minerals in the rocks deep beneath the ice. However, many people think that Antarctica should be left alone, as the last real wilderness on our planet.

The southern part of the world has its winter while the northern part has summer. Polar regions stay dark for the whole day at midwinter, and stay light during the night at midsummer.

Walruses are big blubbery animals with flippers and long tusks, which they use to scrape clams off the seabed. They swim in bitterly cold Arctic waters.

Ships entering **polar waters** must be strengthened so that they can smash their way through floating ice.

The big tails of **whales** are called flukes. Many kinds of whale come to feed in polar waters.

Emperor penguins are Antarctic birds. They cannot fly, but they are excellent swimmers.

Many different kinds of **seal** breed in polar waters. They gather in large numbers on rocks, ice floes, and beaches.

Up to nine tenths of an **iceberg** may be under water. They are a hazard to shipping.

ATLANTIC OCEAN

Permanent Extent of Sea Ice

INDIAN OCEAN

Drake Passage

WEDELL SEA

Antarctic Peninsula

Coats Land

Maud Land

Enderby Land

Ronne Ice Shelf

Cape Darnley

Vinson Massif ▲ 17,744 ft

South Pole ★

GREATER ANTARCTICA

LESSER ANTARCTICA

TRANSANTARCTIC MTNS.

Ross Ice Shelf

Wilkes Land

Erebus 12,444 ft ▲

ROSS SEA

PACIFIC OCEAN

Index

Queensland 57
Rabat 6, 52
Rainbow Bridge 30
rain forests 36, 38, 51, 54
Rangoon 50
Reading 13
Red Sea 7, 42, 43, 53
Red Square 26
Reichstag 17
Reims 15
Republic of Congo 54
Republic of Ireland 12
Reykjavik 6, 8
Rhine river 10, 15, 16
Rhodes 25
Rhône river 14, 15
rice 38, 44, 46, 47, 48, 49, 50
Richmond 31
Rio de Janeiro 6, 39
Rio Grande 6, 30, 31, 34
Rock Springs 30
Rocky mountains 6, 28, 30
Roman Catholic religion 22
Romania 7, 23, 24-25
Rome 6, 7, 20
Ross Sea 61
Rostov 7
Rotterdam 11
Rouen 15
Royal Canadian Mounted Police 29
Russia 5, 7, 8, 22, 26-27, 47, 48
Russian Federation 6, 7, 26-27, 60
Rwanda 55
Saami people 9, 60
St. Basil's Cathedral 26
St. John's 29
St. Kitts 35
St. Lawrence 28, 29, 32
St. Lucia 35
St. Petersburg 7, 26
Sahara desert 7, 52-53
Sahel 52, 53
Salvador 6, 39
Samoa 59
San Antonio 31

San Diego 6, 30
San Francisco 6, 30, 32
San Marino 20, 21
San Salvador 34
Santiago 6, 40
Santorini 25
São Paulo 6, 39
São Tomé & Príncipe 54
Sapporo 5, 7, 48
Sarajevo 24
Sardinia 21
Saudi Arabia 7, 42, 43
Scandinavia 8-9, 60
Scotland 12
Seine river 14, 15
Sendai 5, 49
Senegal 6, 52
Seoul 7, 47
Serbia 24
Severnaya Zemlya 7, 27
Seychelles 55
Shanghai 7, 47
sheep 37, 56, 57, 58
Sheffield 13
Shenyang 7, 47
Shetland islands 12
Shikoku 5, 49
Siberia 7, 27
Sicily 21
Sierra Leone 6, 52
Sierra Madre 6, 34
Sierra Nevada mountains 18
Sikh religion 44
silk 27, 44, 46
Simpson desert 57
Singapore 7, 50, 51
Slovakia 7, 17, 20, 24
Slovak Republic 22, 23, 25
Solomon islands 7, 58
Somalia 53, 55
South Africa 7, 55
South America 4, 6, 36-41
South Australia 57
South China Sea 7, 58
Southeast Asia 50-51
Southern Alps 59
South Island 7, 58, 59
South Korea 7, 46, 47

South Pole 4, 61
Southwest Asia 42-43
Soviet Union 22, 26
Spain 7, 14, 18-19, 33, 38
Spanish language 18, 33, 34, 59
Spanish people 35, 36
spices 45
Sri Lanka 7, 44, 45
Stockholm 7, 9
Strait of Gibraltar 18, 52
Strasberg 15
Stuttgart 16
Sudan 7, 52, 53
Sumatra 50, 51
Surinam 38, 39
Swansea 13
Swaziland 7, 55
Sweden 7, 8, 9
Swiss Alps 16
Switzerland 7, 15, 16, 20
Sydney 7, 56, 57
Syria 7, 42, 43
Taiwan 7, 47
Tajikistan 7, 26
Taj Mahal 45
Tanzania 7, 54, 55
Tashkent 7, 26
Tasmania 7, 56, 57
Tehran 7, 43
Tennessee 31
Texas 31, 32
Thailand 7, 50
Thames river 12, 13
The Grenadines 35
The Gulf 43
The Hague 11
Tibet 7, 44, 46
Tierra del Fuego 40, 41
Tigris river 42, 43
Timbuktu 52
Timor 51, 57
Togo 7, 52
Tokyo 5, 7, 49
Tonga 59
Toronto 6, 29
tourists 15, 17, 18, 50
Tours 14
Transylvanian Alps 24
Trinidad & Tobago 6, 35, 39
Tripoli 7, 53
Tropic of Cancer 6

Tropic of Capricorn 6
tundra 26, 60
Tunisia 7, 53
Turkey 7, 42, 43
Turkmenistan 7, 26
Turks & Caicos islands 35
Tuscany 21
Uele river 7, 55
Uganda 7, 53, 55
Ukraine 7, 22, 24, 26
Uluru 57
United Arab Emirates 7, 42
United Kingdom 7, 12
United States of America 4, 6, 28, 30-33
Uppsala 9
Ural mountains 7, 26
Uruguay 6, 39, 40
Utah 30
Uzbekistan 7
Vancouver 6, 28
Vanuatu 7, 58, 59
Vatican City 6, 20, 21
Venezuela 6, 36, 38, 39
Venice 20
Veracruz 34
Vermont 31
Verona 20
Victoria 57
Victoria Falls 55
Victoria Island 28, 60
Vienna 17
Vietnam 7, 50, 51
Vietnamese people 33
Vilnius 22
Virginia 31
Virgin islands 35
Vladivostok 26, 27
volcano 21, 30, 34,

37, 41, 48, 54
Volga 7, 26
Wales 12, 13
Walloon people 10
Warsaw 22
Washington 6, 30, 31, 32
Wedell Sea 61
Wellington 59
West Africa 33, 35, 52
Western Australia 56
Western Sahara 6, 52
West Frissian islands 10
West Indies 6
West Virginia 31
White Nile river 7, 53
Wilkes Land 61
wine 10, 14, 15, 18, 19, 25
Winnipeg 6, 28
Wisconsin 31
World map 6-7
World Trade Center 32
Wuhan 7, 47
Wyoming 30
Xingu 6
Yakutsk 7, 27
Yellow Sea 7, 47, 58
Yemen 7, 42, 43
Yenisey river 7, 27, 60
Yokohama 5, 49
Yugoslavia 7, 24, 25
Yukon 6, 28, 32
Zagreb 24, 25
Zaire 7
Zambezi river 55
Zambia 7, 55
Zemlya Frantsa Iosifa 7
Zimbabwe 7, 54, 55
Zulu people 54, 55
Zurich 16

Acknowledgments

The publishers wish to thank the artists who have contributed to this book:
Martin Camm, John James, Gill Platt, Terry Riley, Peter Sarson, Roger Smith, Mike White, Alison Winfield

All photographs used in the First Atlas are from MKP Archives